Across The Milestones!

Summerville Press, Inc.
Washington, DC

Published by Summerville Press, Inc.
3254 N Street. N.W.
Washington, DC 20007
(202) 812-2750

E-mail: Summervillemedia@erols.com

Copyright@ 2007 by Summerville Press, Inc.

All rights reserved. No part of this publication may be reproduced or transmitted in any form or by any means, electronic or mechanical, including photocopy, recording or any information storage and retrieval system without permission in writing from the publisher.

Poems written by: Margaret Byrne Heimbold
Book Design by: Smartt Art (www.smartt-art.com)
Photography by: Arthur Heimbold and Annie Schwendinger

ISBN13 978-0-9773961-0-8
ISBN 0-9773961-0-X

Printed in the United States of America

Across The Milestones!

Across The Milestones grew organically from the process of thinking of that which is important. Why do we sometimes ignore milestones? Surprisingly, milestones are occasionally ignored on purpose. Yet, when my muse prodded me to write poems about milestones, I felt compelled to do so. Why? I love acknowledging the rhythm of time and place. It gives me a sense of connection to loved ones and friends, particularly when the very act of acknowledging an important event is received with much happiness.

This chapbook of poems about family, friends, the weather and life is intended to enable us to see the eloquence in the very act of living. Some of the poems are very personal, but their themes are universal. Events that could go by unnoticed are recognized for their importance and necessity. It is my hope that these poems speak to all of us as we find our place in family, society and most of all to find peace within ourselves.

Dedication

As a poet, when I stop to listen to the sound of my own heartbeat, I sometimes hear a stanza and sometimes, I just hear a wonderful line. These opportunities refocus my attention on writing and with the support of my family and friends this chapbook is now in your hands.

Poems help us slow down and feel their tempo. There was a time in my life when its tempo was slowed to the sound of horses' hooves or the swish of bicycle tires on a country road. Both the horse and bicycle dominated our transportation system. We had cars, too, but they were used for long trips and sparingly.

Looking back at that time lived in quiet dignity by people who knew that their pace was muted and measured by timeless expectation, I am grateful for the opportunity to have known a rural life and its seasonal demands. Those memories enabled me to allow the many competing lines of poetry to evolve to their essence. Each poem reflects some of life's moments of pleasure and pain. During readings, I have heard groans of recognition from otherwise non-expressive listeners.

Across the Milestones is dedicated to them and to all whose silence permit poets to use their eloquence as a voice for their expression. It is my hope that this book of poetry provides you with a contented respite as you read and reminisce.

This book of poetry is also dedicated to my husband, children, family and friends. Without their love and support, I would not have known the certainty of pursuing my dream.

Contents

The Age of Innocence
A Place Called Rahugh.............................. 2
The Light in the Sky.................................. 3
A World of Dreams................................... 4
The Freedom To Be.................................. 5
Fortitude... 6

Islands in the Stream
Destiny's Child.. 10
"Just Let Us Be"...................................... 12
"Is Everyone Happy Now?"...................... 13
Memories.. 14
Twilight... 15

Passion to Perseverance
Yesterday.. 18
My Heart... 20
Endurance.. 22
Leap of Faith.. 23
Heaven Sent... 24

Time After Time

Cart Wheeling	28
Isabel	29
Blustery or Blue	30
Vale of Tears	31
Weathering Forces	32

The Persistence of Memory

Forbearance	36
The Price of the Song	38
Never A Mean Word	39
Bitterness	40
Forgiveness	42
Loneliness	44

Milestones

Happy Birthday	48
Loyalty	49
The Journey	50
Mile After Mile	51
New Year's Day	52

The Age Of Innocence

A Place Called Rahugh

A little piece of an earthly place
Where some of us joined the human race.

Contained by an abundance of nature
Unfettered by the geography of a defined creature.

Roads, fields and trees dot a landscape punctuated by hills.
It is simplicity and graciousness without any frills.

People involved in the seven stages of man
Make us pause for a moment and try if we can

To stop, think and measure
The moments of time we treasure.

Whether the birthing of children and burying dead
Is celebrated with joy or lamented with dread.

All the days of our earthly lives
Find workers in search of personal beehives.

The air punctuated with greeting
Fleeting acknowledgements of meeting.

Then the silence surrounds the scene
Of our imagined place in the dream.

The Light in the Sky

The car lights journey to my door made me cry,
Because all the while that I waited,
A teenager's angst soon sated
With country life and away I wanted to fly.

For tomorrow, I would go far away,
And to dream and discover anew,
The meaningful purpose to say,
That the right to my life matters, too.

From my perch at the window I strained,
To imagine that the light in the clouds was for me.
Yet, the color from my face drained,
When the light in the sky didn't stop for me.

It was only an annoying car passing by.

A World of Dreams

Alone in the cool green grass,
A lonely child with a looking glass,
Watching the world of dreams going by,
Fixating on the clouds in the sky.

Enjoying the moments of rare summer sun
Hoping to have some holiday fun.
Because there are no formal holiday plans,
For such children who work as unpaid farm hands.

The Swallow Lake and Juggie's Well, as cool water interludes,
And moments of pleasure-seeking attitudes,
Though as rare as a butterfly's wings beating
The time for holiday pleasure is retreating.

Too soon, will come the howling wind, - only the crackling fire
As cold weather defense, a warm place to retire.
Country living so savored is not for an urban-seeking sense.
Stillness, punctuated by the passing of cars and no nonsense.

Stealing our fantasies 'til out of range of our ears.
Their journey onward a salve for our imagined fears.
Creaking bicycles in need of oil and attention.
A reminder of country folk's reduced financial dimension.

The Freedom To Be

*Families, fields and roads form the community.
Representing the ideal of societal unity.
Freedom is granted or withheld at will.
Because the price of living here part of life's bill.*

*Those within the community are restored by faith and hope.
Their promise is to obey, comply and cope
If they choose to leave and go away,
They will be welcome here again someday.*

*Fields beckon farmers and visitors with their abundance
And children absorb the messages of dutiful attendance.
Chores must be done according to the season.
Their completion beyond question and reason.*

*Roads firmly advancing those hastening to town.
While others depart to earn the cap and gown.
Each road providing access and opportunity
To the eclectic imaginations of those in the community.*

Fortitude

You are a shining example of fortitude,
Rising above life's challenging platitude.
Observing necessity with compassion.
Your kindness is always in fashion.

Influenced by cleansing water,
Journeying to destinations without falter.
Thousands of miles you have traveled
On memories and roads not yet graveled.

Each uphill climb, you embraced,
Not fully knowing what you faced.
So many counted on your generosity
Which you granted without pomposity.

Measuring the moments of reflected glory,
Each family member and friend has a story
Of your good humor, vision and creativity
Exhibited lovingly, expansively and with sensitivity.

Your recent health trials behind you now,
Looking forward to a new life with unfurrowed brow.
We are happy that you are blessed with good news
Afforded with prayers, spoken on knees, in church pews.

Weathering this difficult uncertain storm
Its outcome for your enthusiasm has been reborn.
True to your nature of strength without measure
Enhances the good health you can now treasure.

Islands In The Stream

Destiny's Child

Mary, as we look at you face
And see the determination of the human race.
Knowing that your life's journey
Had some times been on the gurney.

Each birth of the progeny of your thighs
Brought forth thru pain and grateful sighs.
All six sons were named for kings
And expected to do great things.

Birthed as a child in a foreign land
Comforted by your immigrant parent's hand.
Your exceptional journey's transformations
Were expressed by moments of exquisite formations.

Working, living and tending those who needed your support
Challenged your medical, maternal and balanced comport.
Nursing was your chosen vocational calling.
Your maternal support stopped your children from falling.

You've carried your senior years with dignity.
And we watched you closely for signs of our destiny.
Seeing you now fragile, vulnerable and lost to us.
Makes us slow to respond to life's fuss.

Holding your hand enables us to feel your presence.
Not yet fathoming your loss or essence.
Dreading the day when God calls you home.
Leaving us here to face life alone.

Yet, grateful for been gifted by your love
And counting on your prayers from above.

"Just Let Us Be"

Families, ebbing and flowing with emotional strain,
Sometimes not knowing what words to refrain.
Yet, patient smiles masking the disappointment of pain,
In a life filled with expectation and so much to gain.

Born to please, and not knowing where to begin,
Each parent expecting excellent versions of her and of him.
When the grandparents look over their brood,
They wonder how many beyond one breaks the mood?

If three generations can face each with latitude,
Remaining in concert with each other's attitude.
Where else can we find experience laced with lassitude,
Tempered with love and the restraining words of rectitude?

As our eyes and minds journey to the need to know.
Our parents and grandparents learn when to let go.
Heartbreaking and warming for all to see,
Our lives resonate: "Just let us be."

"Is Everyone Happy Now?"

She drives her little red car often and fast.
And is healthy as a horse with genetics that last.
My mother is an example of life worth living
Each day she has focused on the joy of giving.

All who know her admire her love of Bingo.
She delves into crises with a bemused lingo.
No one is a stranger necessary to fathom.
All are friends of an equal atom.

Her children uneven, and admired
Observe that she never lets life leave her mired.
Always forward looking and thinking,
She has embraced life without shrinking.

With an extended family of responsibilities,
She has only known the many possibilities.
To each and everyone whom she is glad to know.
The question is always the same "Is everyone happy now?"

Memories

Mother, as I try to recall
The fleeting promise of it all
I see you alone in your shell
Imprisoned by memories of wartime hell.

You showed moments of the girl beneath,
Surging forward in your pretty sheath.
But, motherhood in trying times
Reduced your enjoyment of favorite pastimes.

Only later did I know your love of music and art
And saw glimpses of your loving heart.
Memories of your warm hand and countenance
Enrich recollections of my childhood sustenance.

Now I am journeying on a smoother path
Where you, sadly, doth not hath.
My gift to you in my moments of reflection
Is to set you free from my introspection.

May the freedom of song and art
Set you soaring with wings from my heart.
Then, I will ponder your life for a while
Warmed by the presence of your happy smile.

Twilight

*Glorious light of your mother's life
Led away with drum and fife.
Lonely that she left us on the day
That we also celebrated your birthday.*

*Still fathoming the pain of your loss
And the soothing calm of your mother's voice.
In the memory book of longing
We are seeking the solace of belonging.*

*You will be admired for your loving care
Of a mother who choose to dare
The celebration of evening's arrival
By toasting another day of happy survival.*

*Taking away the journey of ending
And traveling the road of sending
A prayer, a poem, the warmth of sunlight
In whose flourishes, we all delight.*

*But, now that your mother has left this place.
With the pain of her loss on your tear stained face.
Taking heart that her maternal vigilance
Is still observed from heaven with diligence.*

Passion to Perseverance

Yesterday

No more can we resolve the past
And the promises the future will last.
Our purpose here has been done
And our love gave life to a son.

We struggled and wrestled with our inabilities
And tried to transcend our capabilities.
Our reservoir of differences insurmountable
And yet to society we were accountable.

Where did the hope and joy go?
Who was the stranger we did not know.
You with your entrenched immutability
Or me with my inscrutability.

Too young to ask or bear the pain.
Too humble to endure the mistake of shame.
Too strong to admit the blame
What happened extinguished the flame.

Counting the moments of regret
The path and speed had been set
To a future of painful upset
Of recourse, and plans with no button to reset.

*Till now we stop to say goodbye
Its fleeting memory makes me cry.
For a time when life stood still
And the future was all uphill.*

*Uphill it is even today
The course still has a lot to say
Of life's bitter burdens and moments to pay
And I am lost for words to relay.*

*Good bye to the challenges of yesterday
And move on to the possibilities of today
To a time full of anticipated harmony
Where the past and future are in symphony.*

My Heart

A glimpse of recognition, then painful indecision
Life becomes complicated
Sifting through the possibilities
Trying hard to avoid the realities.

Falling in love beyond my scope.
Yet, feeling the beginnings of hope.
Years spent in aimless despair
Seems to suggest life now will repair.

The outward appearance pleasing and exciting
Eyes twinkling with opportunity, inviting
To a future of uncertain innuendo.
My emotions sashaying to the beat of Nintendo.

Short of breath with anticipation
A corner is turned with elation
Curly hair and heartfelt eyes
Satisfy my cynical intuitive spies.

Not looking for a soul mate
Yet, open to the opportunity not to hate
A perfectly wonderful man
Who strives to reach this frozen-hearted woman.

Our chemistry is an electric mix of love and need
Which we tried desperately not to heed
(Its promise full of endless possibility)
Because we were steeped in necessary civility.

Pained by the reality of our circumstance
Buoyed by the chance to achieve sustenance
In lives fragmented by regret
We moved forward past pain and the need to forget.

Your black hair, brown eyes and frown
Were the end of a birthing crown.
Gladly all of that became blonde hair and blue eyes
Confirming a relationship to your family ties.

A son to call my own,
And a child to count on when you are grown.
The journey has been interrupted with physical pain.
Who knew that a genetic flaw would slow your life's gain?

You've lived your dreams to the fullest.
And, no you have never been the dullest.
As you embarked on the journey of your own
Visioning safety in conquests unknown,

No moment of life has surpassed
Your energy, struggle and experiences amassed.
To make me as proud as a mother can be.
A journey of hope and optimistic legacy.

Leap of Faith

For each moment in time
Every wish was for a daughter of mine.
Then one day out of the dew
All the signs pointed to you.

You seemed so self-sufficient and strong.
I now know that assumption was wrong.
We threw away all of our hesitation
And embarked on a journey of endless gestation.

To Russia we had to go
And bring you back to a home that you did not know.
Everyday, a process of discovery,
Of fragmented language bits and memory.

Never needing to know more than you can say,
For you, our daughter, are home to stay.

Heaven Sent

In snowy March to Russia we went,
To bring home our daughter who was heaven sent.
For nine months we have been busy bees,
Adjusting to life with far fewer golf tees.

Our rewards are a daughter, who blossoms daily,
And we report her progress with missives so gaily.
Who knew that Victoria would grace us with her wit,
Kind heart, quick mind and be the neighborhood hit?

These twenty months have flown by,
Each day is filled with the words of "please try."
To comfort a daughter whose struggle is obvious,
Sustains us now through her being endlessly curious.

What we had taken for granted
Is now exciting and new.
We look at life differently, not slanted
Makes this joyful experience pure and true.

Time After Time

Cart Wheeling

Mary, I remember you when,
Cart wheeling over the golf course glen,
You celebrated each good drive
With a gusto that deserved a high-five.

You enjoyed professional accomplishments.
But, being a wife and mother are your preferred achievements.
Jimmy and Christopher bask in your caring presence,
While you know, that your family reflects your quintessence.

Through the years, we measured birthdays
With pretty cards and grateful days.
And now we are happy for the reminders
Our lives recorded in photo binders.

When we need to reach across time,
It calls for a poem to fulfill a rhyme.
The happy recollection of your optimism
Calling forth from life's well-lived prism.

If you want to cartwheel again
Over the shadows of life's glen,
We want to be there with you
As we recount the days of skies so blue.

Isabel

Isabel, you've created quite a roar.
Making us wonder what you had in store.
Wind monitors proving your worth.
Television reporters in slickers offer astonished mirth.

When did the following of weather so fearfully,
Become a pastime observed so cheerfully?
Isabel, now your power and strength are slowing
And you are leaving without our knowing.

Did you come to say hello?
When are we sure you must go?
The preparation and reporting was extensive,
And the investment in cleanup expensive.

Listeners and viewers must be entertained.
And all you left is evidence it rained.
But now we know that you cut quite a swath
Of downed trees and power lines in our path.

Some rivers are swollen and spilling their contents.
Small business owners are full of laments.
So, Isabel, you created quite a roar
And now, we sadly know what was in store.

Blustery or Blue

Comments are rampant no matter what weather type,
Some are unfazed by the hype.
For them rain is an excruciating event
Yet, for the farmer in spring it is heaven sent.

Slashing cats and dogs it is.
The images beyond metamorphosis
When the sun surprises for a moment,
Its comings and goings deserve full comment.

Weather is an exhaustive universal topic
Consuming an entire television channel's microscopic.
Each network news hours is never complete
Without the necessary maps to be replete.

So the weather serves a useful purpose
Inviting us all to on occasional repose
Whether for rain or sunshine we rest
We are enabled to take the weather's test.

Vale of Tears

*Tom, tears to do not wash away
All the memories of yesterday.
But, now we are left to cope
With the loss of a life so full of hope.*

*Go free to enjoy flowers of lavender and white.
And cars whose power and might.
Made you happiest with the wind on your face
Ending the pain of the human race.*

*We know you have joined your Mom and Dad
Leaving your family so very sad.
Pray for them here in this vale of tears
And ask God to take away Eric's fears.*

*May God welcome you to his heavenly place
And bless you now with a smile on his face.*

Weathering Forces

The weather has us all on a tether,
Tied to life's ebbs and flows.

We can't control the wind's history.
Calling its effusiveness a mystery.
Directions make us listen and consider
If their purpose is to make us shiver.

The notion of a ferocious tornado
Disrupts our lives of intended bravado.
Waves washing over our emotions
As we envision the bottomless oceans.

Silent in their delivery of messages,
But, beckoning our fantasy passages.
The weather never ends our dialogue,
Yet, it often controls our monologue.

The Persistence of Memory

Forbearance

Bob, what we will we do now
That you are no longer here
To teach us the how
Of making this life clear?

Where will we look
To find your friendly face
And read life's necessary book
On the importance of pace?

Why did you not deride
Your crushing physical woes
But, instead chose to stride
Along a fuller path on optimistic toes?

When did God so wisely surmise
That a man of your character was a gift?
Taking you away now, a surprise
The pain from which we feel so bereft.

*How will we carry on
In life's valley of loss of hope?
Our hearts ache that you are gone
And pray for God's grace to cope.*

*Yes, we will honor your life
By wrapping our love around your family.
We will look out for Patty, John and Charles
And know you composed life's precious simile.*

*So, goodbye for a while, our friend
With these soulful poetic messages
We will try to adequately append
The eloquence of your life's passages.*

The Price of the Song

Your birth was a lifetime thrill,
Your dimples and helplessness part of God's will.

The years of first teeth and trainers a new experience for sure
Each day was a revelation of the need for more.

As the teenage years unfolded in opacity
Reducing my role of fatherly capacity.

It's the pain of now being coldly ignored
Or are you avoiding the trouble of being bored?

Wondering where it all went wrong
Other fathers tell me it's the bitter price of the song.

Never A Mean Word

Aunt Mimi, you made us proud as a family can be
Your love and achievements for all to see.
Shining examples of a life well lived
A beacon of faith, in God you believed.

Now we must say goodbye for a while
And soon we will again see your beautiful smile.
How lucky we are to have been loved by you.
Your many ministrations came out of the blue.

Each one will recall your compassion and kindness
And note your outstanding clear mindedness.
When it came to academics or bridge you just soared.
But, your answers were never roared.

No one could match your outstanding ability
You just quietly used your brilliant facility.
When God gave out unconditional love,
Your patience and sensitivity resonated from above.

Now as we send you away
To God's promised garden to play.
Pray for us as we tearfully recall
The fleeting moments of it all.

Bitterness

Bitterness came to visit our family.
Its mantra laced with hostility.
Hateful voices began to fester
Using words to grievously pester.

Bitterness left behind a loving past
And now it looks like it might last.
Beyond wishful hope and reason,
Its fulfillment appears in full season.

The years have taken their price.
No one, it seems, wants to be nice.
Each has given themselves permission
To pursue this search and destroy mission.

Memories once treasured are now trashed.
To heal open wounds, the future is dashed.
In a hodge podge of righteous recrimination.
Goodness is bathed in sinister accusation.

*Yet, each hurt and angry family member
Is capable of the chance to remember
Their reason for these painful decisions
To tear each other with emotional incisions.*

*Yesterday's healing chance is lost to futility.
Assess today's potential for opportunity.
Lay open time with its unrelenting pain.
Discover tomorrow's other path to healing gain.*

*Send bitterness far, far away.
Let the wisdom of all sides come out to play.
Gently allow each other to rewrite
The disappointment of this disabling plight.*

*Look at the past with forgiveness.
Where hearts hold no bitterness.
Allow memories of leavened introspective
Create the balm of soothing perspective.*

Forgiveness

Noticing the cruelty of passing time.
Focusing on memories in relief sublime.
Willing to trade the elegance of subtleties
For the earnestness of harsh realities.

How did we know that it mattered
Or how did we know that we cared
Was it our own life's experiences
Or just those that we shared.

When we stop at each path to discover
If we are there to try to recover
The opportunity to do it all again
By delivering our memories from relentless refrain.

The kaleidoscope of fragmented memories.
Leaves us with the eternal mix of journeys
That could have taken us in any direction.
But would we look back now with abject affection.

Each face moves in concert with expectation.
The joys, the sorrows etched in mutation
No time to turn back the marching clock
But to walk the path in a smashing frock.

Live life fully and with passion.
Throw away the difficulty of confusion.
Make our moments matter with perseverance
So that those left behind can note with reverence.

Take the elegance, experience and emotion
Match them to the moments of life's potion
When this day is done note it with attitude
Because tomorrow should be met with gratitude.

Loneliness

There it goes again, the shock, the fear
Gasping for breath and the feeling of death so near.

What creates this anxiety
A child's helplessness or imagined deity?

Or was it the loss of a mother's or father's voice
With no event or birthday to rejoice?

The years have filtered the pain
But flashbacks are a fragmented refrain.

What ghostly figure of impending doom
Created this helpless child's gloom?

Milestones

Happy Birthday

It's the cheerful voice of perpetual kindness
Propelled by a unique clear mindedness
That attracts us to Lynda with gratitude
Because who else do you know with such attitude?

Over the years, I have sometimes shed tears
At her unfailing wisdoms to quell all my fears.
As we look around the room at each other
We know that Lynda has been our earth Mother.

From her many obvious talents to calligraphy
We wait as she travels the geography
To learn once again, the loss of her being away
But now, we have so much more to say.

We're here because Lynda you never forget
That each person is a new friend you've just met
You take time to stop, enjoy and celebrate
So, that's why it's appropriate we congregate.

So here we are, aware of how much you mean to us
And only Lynda is wondering why all the fuss.
Let's raise a glass, write a poem, and savor the moment
Because, Lynda, you are reason for this merriment.

Loyalty

For well over forty years,
Whether thru laughter or some tears,
We've shared a supportive friendship
Which has always steadied my ship.

Your counsel and wise words
Were essential during times of no forewords.
Their value necessary, not just to me,
Served as an example for all to see.

Today, you are recognized justifiably,
By those whom you've befriended so admirably.
The Headless Horseman is a crowning glory
Of recognition and achievement for your history.

Family has been your comforting source
And this recognition will honor them as a force.
Elaine, Danny and Lauren your supporting crew,
With spouses, and grandchildren to create life anew.

Their support for you has been your strength
So, let's raise a toast, to their energies well spent.
Elaine, Lauren, Peter, Emily, Joseph, Danny and Christina,
Have all added immeasurably to your life's patina.

Sleepy Hollow has also been a special part,
Of a man whose strength is his lion heart.
For old friends like us, this is the Dan we know.
Your many friends are examples of friendship too numerous to show.

The Journey

Life is a unique discovery for all of us.
Not always clear, but sometimes made tenuous.

Try as we engage in the endless might
To figure someone else's plight,
The message is always lost,
On the others, except for the host.

Painful as it seems,
We watch our elders give up their dreams.
Terrifying to us whose journey is still in progress.
No matter what the pain, we would not want less.

As we embrace the telling seasons,
Burdened or lightened by life's lessons.
A reminder that we are journeying together
But, yet, the trip feels like a moment of discordant meter.

Our middle years poignant with the awareness of time
Both children and parents are responsibilities in rhyme.

To reach inside and find an inner child
Free of the intensity of expressions so mild
Journeying onward, we feel the inevitable pinch
Of life's path shortening inch by inch.

Mile After Mile

*Jonah, the first thing we notice is your happy smile.
Then, we learn of your running mile after mile.
Sometimes, we even imagine that both are related
Because we assume that your creative energies are sated.*

*Marathons and missions the measurements of your anima.
Milestones and miracles are a tribute to your stamina.
Your laughter echoes through each happy event
And your uplifting spirit increases all merriment.*

*Jonah, you are truly our national treasure
With attributes too numerous to measure.
Yet, if we pause for a moment to surmise
The results of your efforts are no surprise.*

*Your multifaceted career of corporate complexity
Is enhanced by your boundless intellectual capacity.
Your achievement of management challenges never did daunt
And yet your successes, you never do flaunt.*

*So, let's raise a glass and make a toast
To Jonah, the reason for this wonderful roast.
On your birthday, only your family and friends can boast
Of Jonah, our friend, the man that we love the most.*

New Year's Day

A brand new beginning with promises to say.
Turning a page to keep some reflections at bay.
Full of anticipation, we wonder anew what to expect
Mindful of experiences we've come to respect.

Each year, reaching out to family and friends dominate
Our conscious desires with time to ruminate.
Shared journeys enriched with the preciousness of time.
We surmise future opportunities with satisfaction sublime.

The wish lists are shorter because of our wisdom.
Drawing us closer to the demands of the kingdom.
Searching for balance amidst the striving and improvement.
We seek to bring peace to our goals for achievement.

What does this New Year say to us
When the world is in a state of eternal crisis?
Turning on the news brings us endless analysis
Of people, places and threats too numerous.

*Casting our eyes at the chance for a New Year.
Beckoning us to uphold our values so dear.
Yet, knowing our example will lead some
To exhibit their disapproval with a denial of our freedom.*

*In the cacophony of a new world order.
Let us pause to express generosity necessitated by our brother.
These lessons are universal with intense import.
Lend them to our purpose and promise to support.*

*Try to do what we can for our fellowman
Whether as a private or global citizen.
This defined space and time,
Our journey and sustenance perceived by each as mine*